WITHDRAWN

Take Care of Yourself

Staying Safe in the Sun

Siân Smith

Heinemann
LIBRARY

Chicago, Illinois

www.capstonepub.com

Visit our website to find out more information about Heinemann-Raintree books.

To order:

☎ Phone 800-747-4992

▧ Visit www.capstonepub.com
to browse our catalog and order online.

Edited by Dan Nunn, Rebecca Rissman,
   and John-Paul Wilkins
Designed by Victoria Allen
Picture research by Tracy Cummins
Production by Alison Parsons
Originated by Capstone Global Library Ltd
Printed and bound in China by Leo Paper Products Ltd

16 15 14 13 12
10 9 8 7 6 5 4 3 2 1

Library of Congress Cataloging-in-Publication Data
Smith, Siân.
   Staying safe in the sun / Siân Smith.
      p. cm.—(Take care of yourself!)
   Includes bibliographical references and index.
   ISBN 978-1-4329-6712-3 (hb)—ISBN 978-1-4329-6719-2 (pb)
   1. Skin—Care and hygiene—Juvenile literature. I. Title.
   RL87.S63 2013
   616.5—dc23   2011049841

Acknowledgments
We would like to thank the following for permission to reproduce photographs: Capstone Library pp. 15, 23b (Karon Dubke); Corbis pp. 11, 12, 23c (© Randy Faris); Dreamstime.com p. 22a (© Hunk); Getty Images p. 16 (Photolibrary); istockphoto pp. 6 (© Joel Carillet), 9 (© Jo Ann Snover), 14, 22d (© mark wragg), 18 (© Wilson Valentin), 19 (© Linda Epstein), 20 (© Marilyn Nieves); Shutterstock pp. 4 (© holbox), 5 (© Yuriy Kulyk), 7 (© AISPIX), 8 (© Rob Marmion), 10 (© Dubova), 13, 17 (© MaszaS), 21, 23a (© wavebreakmedia ltd), 22b (© Teeratas), 22c (© Marek R. Swadzba).

Front cover photograph of Hispanic mother rubbing sunscreen on her daughter at the beach reproduced with permission of Getty Images (Erik Isakson). Rear cover photograph of family on a cruise ship reproduced with permission of Shutterstock (© Rob Marmion).

Every effort has been made to contact copyright holders of material reproduced in this book. Any omissions will be rectified in subsequent printings if notice is given to the publisher.

We would like to thank Nancy Harris and Dee Reid for their assistance in the preparation of this book.

Contents

Sunshine

A little bit of sunshine is good
for our bodies.

But the sun is hot and powerful.

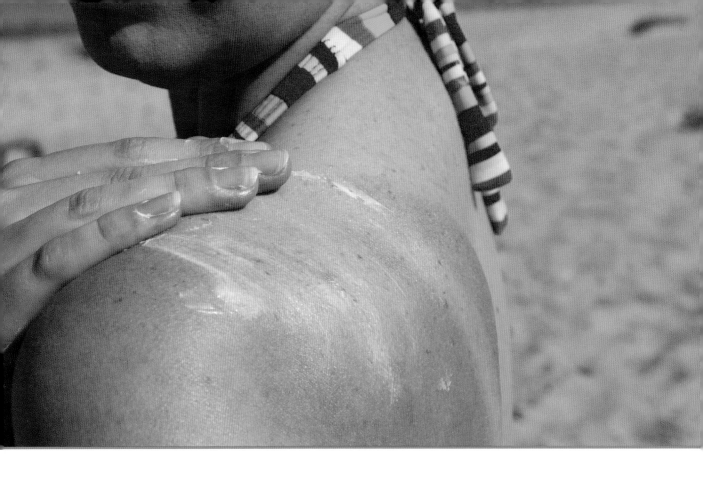

Too much sunshine can hurt
our bodies.

You can have fun in the sun, but
you must stay safe in it, too.

Keep Your Eyes Safe

On sunny days, wear sunglasses
to keep your eyes safe.

Never look right at the sun,
even with sunglasses.

On Sunny Days

On sunny days, put sunscreen on your skin to keep it safe.

Don't forget your ears and
your nose!

Put on more sunscreen after
a few hours.

If your sunscreen washes off,
put more on.

Sunscreens with high numbers keep you safer.

Sunblock keeps your nose
and cheeks safe. It comes in
bright colors.

sleeve

You can wear a top with sleeves to keep your arms safe.

You can wear white clothes to keep you cooler.

You can wear a hat to keep
your head safe.

There are lots of different hats
you can try.

When the weather is hot,
drink lots of water.

Don't stay in the sunshine too long.
Find some shade if you can.

Name Game

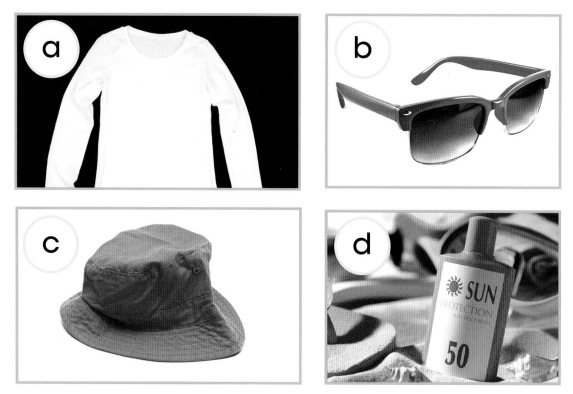

Can you name these things? They help you to stay safe in the sun.

Answers on page 24

Picture Glossary

 **shade** cool place away from strong sunlight

 **sunblock** special cream you use to block the sun. Some sunblock comes in bright colors.

 **sunscreen** special cream you use to stay safe in the sun

Index

Answers to question on page 22
a = white top   b = sunglasses
c = hat   d = sunscreen

Notes for parents and teachers

Before reading

Talk with the children about different ways of keeping our bodies safe. Find out what they know about staying safe in the sun. What do they do to keep their bodies safe? Bring in or show them pictures of different sunscreens. Do they know what the numbers mean? Explain that sunscreens with higher numbers give us more protection from the sun.

After reading

• With the children, list all the things you can do to help you to stay safe in the sun. Play a memory game in groups. Start the game by saying, "When I go out in the sun I…" and then choose a way of staying safe in the sun. For example, you could wear sunglasses, wear sunscreen, wear sunblock, wear a hat, move to the shade when hot, or drink lots of water. Take turns to repeat what has been said so far and to add another way of staying safe in the sun.

• Reinforce techniques for staying safe in the sun by helping the children to design posters that show others how to stay safe. If a digital camera is available, children could take photos of items that help them to stay safe to use in their posters.